PHP

A Step By Step Guide from Beginner to Expert (Learn PHP in 2 Hours and Start Programming Today)

ALEXANDER CLYDE

D1416486

TABLE OF CONTENTS

PHP

A BRIEF HISTORY OF PHP

Like the freest software, PHP belongs to the community. A large number of people have helped throughout his life to creating both the core language and the huge number of bookstores available. However, we must attribute his creation originally to Rasmus Lerdorf, creator of the language in 1994.

PHP was born as a CGI written in C that allowed the interpretation of a limited number of commands. The system was named Personal Home Page Tools and acquired relative achievement because other people asked Rasmus to enable them to use their programs on their pages. Given the permission of the first PHP and additionally, its creator created a system to process forms to which he assigned the name of FI (Form Interpreter) and the bearing of these two tools, it would be the original compact version of the language: PHP /FI.

The next major participation to the language was made in mid-97 when the parser was reprogrammed; new features such as aid for new Internet protocols and support for the vast majority of commercial databases were included. All these improvements laid the foundations for PHP version 3. Although at that time the language had a long way to go to become an indispensable tool, it integrated a large number of functionalities "from home," so that its community of programmers it was growing, attracted by its usefulness and the ease to start developing websites.

PHP in its version 4 incorporated as a novelty the "Zend" engine, developed with greater meditation to cover the needs of that moment and solve some difficulties of the previous version. Some improvements of this latest version are its speed thanks to the experience that it is first compiled and then executed, whereas ere it was executed while the code was being interpreted, its greater independence from the web server performing native versions of PHP for more platforms and a further elaborate API with more functions.

However, the final maturity of PHP came with version 5, which remained in the market for more than 11 years and is still in maintenance today. The main novelty of version 5 was an improved integration of the Object Oriented Programming paradigm.

Note: Although the PHP 4 version already had tools for programming with objects, these were very rudimentary and did not respond to the needs of the developers, nor were they comparable in power and possibilities to other languages. PHP, in its intention to serve both experienced programmers and developers starting from scratch, still incorporates the possibility of developing with or without object-oriented programming.

During all the years of PHP 5 life, there were many changes. Many tools were added to the language, allowing doing things that were highly demanded by the developers and that other newer language had incorporated output. One of the clearest examples was the autoload of classes, which allowed the incorporation of the package manager Composer.

However, 11 years with the same version suggested that the language had stalled and PHP was losing adherents, although in statistical terms, number of developers and labor demand, its superiority is still overwhelming. Between all that time, several situations did not come to submit PHP 6 and finally the community decided to skip that version number and launch PHP 7 directly.

PHP 7 today is a reality. The improvements in performance are very remarkable and have again placed the language among the most powerful. It is available in the number of servers, but its adoption is still not total. The reason is that PHP has lots of libraries and software that has not been fully updated or that throws errors when running under that new version. In the next months or years, the situation will change because PHP 7 is very desirable for any project.

Servers with PHP

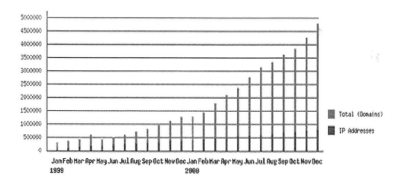

Graph of the number of domains and IP addresses that use PHP.

Netcraft statistics

Although this image is something old, it indicates that the number of servers that use PHP has exploded, which shows that PHP is a very popular technology. This is due; among other causes that PHP is the ideal complement for the Linux-Apache tandem to be compatible with server-side programming of websites. Thanks to the acceptance that has been achieved, and the great efforts made by a growing community of collaborators to perform it most optimally, we can ensure that the language will enhance a standard that will share the achievements augured to the set of systems originated in open source.

To this day, few tools among the most used for the development of web sites or applications are not made with PHP. WordPress, Drupal, Magento, Prestashop, etc. They are examples of this. This trend does not stop growing, but now we have to add a huge amount of frameworks such as Symfony, Laravel or Zend, which have allowed PHP to become an even more powerful, productive language capable of implementing best practices for the health of the projects.

PHP community

Also, the developer community that uses PHP has evolved a lot. Many of the professionals who have been using this language over the years have grown, professionally and naturally, next to PHP. We can say that PHP has been and continues to be the cause of its success or professional sustenance.

That maturity of the developers has also been important for the language. In its beginnings, the community was attracted to PHP for its amount of utilities and the ease with which to start working. However, people did not care so much about aspects such as security or maintainability of applications. Today the community is aware of the importance of robust and scalable platforms, and this has allowed PHP to take a professional turn. Much of that transformation is due to the frameworks above and the ability of PHP to absorb and bring to itself the best of other languages.

In the PHP Manual, you will learn to take your first steps with the language, but we want you not to stay there and continue to strive to learn more and more. In DesarrolloWeb.com amount of material, you have to keep growing, as manual object-oriented programming in PHP 5, the Manual Composer or frameworks like laravel. Being rigorous with your work and how you use language is the best favor you will give to the community and yourself as a professional.

WHAT IS PHP?

PHP (PHP recursive acronym: Hypertext Preprocessor) is a very popular open source language especially suitable for web development, and that can be embedded in HTML.

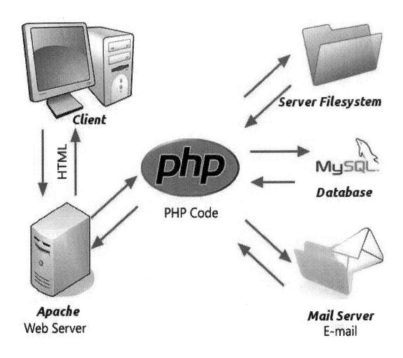

Good, but what does it mean? An example will clarify things:

Example # 1 An introductory example

<!DOCTYPE html>

<html>

```
<head>

  <title>Ejemplo</title>

</head>

<body>


  <?php

    echo "¡Hola, soy un script de PHP!";

  ?>


</body>

</html>
```

Instead of using many commands to display HTML (as in C or Perl), PHP pages consists of HTML with embedded code that does "something" (in this case, display "Hello, I'm a PHP script!). PHP code is enclosed between the special tags start and end <?phpand?> allowing entering and exiting the "PHP mode".

What distinguishes PHP from something on the client side like Javascript is that the code is executed on the server, generating HTML and sending it to the client. The client will receive the result of executing the script, although the underlying code that it was will not be known. The web server can even be configured to process all HTML files with PHP, so there is no alternative for users to know what's up to their sleeve.

The best thing about using PHP is its extreme simplicity for the beginner, but at the very time, it offers many advanced features for professional programmers. Do not be afraid to read the long list of PHP features. In a few hours, you can start writing your first scripts.

Although PHP development is focused on scripting server-side scripts, it can be used for many other things. Read on and discover more in the section what can PHP do? , or go directly to the introductory tutorial if you are only interested in web programming.

PHP FUNCTIONS

Function: it is an independent subroutine that performs a much defined operation, which we can use many times from our code. This means a more readable, compact and easy to debug code, since within our script we will only have the call to the function and the function itself will be external (another file or library), or it will be in a part of the script destined to that function.

External function: the definition of the function can be done outside the script and stored in an external library; in this way, it will be accessible to all programs.

Internal function: the definition of the function is done within the script or script in this way it will be accessible from any point of the same program, but external programs will not be able to make use of it.

```
functions 2.php - Free Script Editor

File   Edit   View   Convert   Search   Insert   Tools   Help

1172
1173
1174
1175        if ( is_singular() && ! is_home() && ! is_page
        page.php' ) )
1176
1177           $classes[] = 'singular';
1178
1179
1180
1181        return $classes;
1182
1183    }
1184
1185    add_filter( 'body_class', 'twentyeleven_body_cla:
1186
1187
1188    add_post_type_support( 'page', 'excerpt' );
1189
1190
1191
1192
1193
```

When we need a function, we will use it by making a call by its specific name. In occasions the function also receives values, these will be placed in parentheses and are called parameters.

After the function has been executed, it returns a result to the calling program; this result is called return value or function value.

// Syntax of a function with parameter step

```php
function functionName ( $ parameter1 , $ parameter2 ) {

    // Expression

        // Return parameter value

    return $ parameter_1 + $ parameter_2 ;

}

$ parameter_1 = 4;

$ parameter_2 = 2;

        // Call the function exactly with the same name

    echo 'Add parameters ='. FunctionName ( $ parameter_1 , $ parameter2 );

    // Return 6
```

Function with parameter passing

Result returned by the function with parameter step.

Sum parameters = 6

Function with parameter passing

```php
// Syntax of a function without parameters

function sinParameters () {

    $ var_1 = 4 ;

    $ var_2 = 2 ;

        // Sum of variables
```

```php
$ result = $ var_1 + $ var_2 ;

    echo 'The sum of the variables ='. $ result ; // Return 6

}
```

```php
// Call to function

sinParameters () ;

The sum of the variables = 6
```

The name of a function must not start with the dollar symbol ($); it must be a unique name. Although function names are not case-sensitive, it is advisable to be consistent in naming the function with the same name with which it was called.

The parameters are visual and go between the paraments and separated by a comma (,).

The return statement is obvi- ous since the function can, in some cases, return a value or perform any given action without the need to return any value.

Function types

PHP functions are classified into three types:

- Natives of the language
- Language extension

- Defined by the user

Native language functions: are those used with matrices and strings.

Go up

Language extension functions: We can find them in extension libraries, and they are not installed in the basic configuration of PHP. When being in libraries, some extensions are installed by default, although others have to be installed in the system in a specific way.

Go up

User-defined functions: These are the functions that we create as users; they are customized to solve the problem of our code.

Go up

Definition of functions

Function defined in the main code

We can define a function among the rest of the main code; the position of the definition of the function can be in any part of the main code, both behind and behind the position in which it is called. If we define a function and it is not used, nothing happens; it will only be executed when we have a call.

Functions defined within a condition

If we define a function within a conditional b, lock if (), it cannot be called if the condition in which the function is defined is not fulfilled.

The function defined within another function

If we define function_2 within function_2 function_1, theYou cannot run if it has not been called before the función_1.

Go up

Parameters of the function

A function can receive three types of parameters

Passed by value

Passed by reference

Defaults

Passed by value: predetermine and more secure way to pass parameters to the function, the parameters arrive at the function as a copy of the variable passed as a parameter, which means that the variable will change the value in the execution of the function, but the value of the original variable will not change.

```php
// Passed by value

$ byValue = 100 ;


echo "Initial value of \ $ byValue : $ byValue <br />";


// Function call with parameter step by

test value ( $ byValue );



 // Modify the value of the test

 function parameter ( $ byValue ) {


    echo "Value of \ $ byValue within function: $ byValue <br />";
    // Still the same value


    $ perValue = 200 ; // We change the value of $ byValue


    // Modified value

    echo " Value of \ $ by Value modified within the function: $ byValue <br />";
```

```
}
```

Initial value of $ per Value outside the function: 100

Value of $ per Value within the function: 100

Value of $ per Value modified within the function: 200

Go up

Passed by reference: the passed variable will not be a copy of the calling code variable but the variable itself will be the one that passes. This way of passing parameters will be fine when we want the variable passed as a parameter to change the value automatically in the calling code variable.

To use the step by reference, we will put the symbol ampersand & in front of the parameter of the function, this will make PHP interpret that the parameter occupies the same address as the calling code variable, it will be like an "alias" inside the function.

NOTE: Since PHP 6 objects are passed by reference without the need to do so explicitly.

We will take special care with the use of parameters, because if the calling code contains 2 parameters, the function will also have 2 parameters, never less, if not, PHP 6 will produce a warning message, activated from the php.ini file by activating error_reporting. One way to ignore this warning is to place the at sign (@) in front of the calling code (expression).

In case the function had more parameters than the call, PHP 6 would not produce any type of message or warning, only the attributes that exceed are ignored.

// Parameter passed by reference (&)

// Function (lowercase name)

function byReference (& $ var) {

    // Multiplied value of $ x for 2

    $ var = $ var * 2;

    echo " Value of $ x passed by reference =". $ var ;

}

```php
// Variable is worth 100

$ x = 100;

echo " Initial value of $ x =". $ x ;
```

```php
// Call function (name in upper case)

PORREFERENCIA ( $ x ); // Now it's worth 200
```

Initial value of $ x = 100

Value of $ x passed by reference = 200

Go up

Default parameters: It is a matter of passing as a parameter a variable with a constant value, which we declare between the parentheses of the same function. The default worth must be a constant expression, never a variable, a member of a class or a call to a function.

```php
// Default parameters

// The declared constant is placed at the end

function schedule ( $ peachepe , $ achetemele = "HTML" ) {
```

```
    return "To know how to program with $ achetemele and $
peachepe .";



}



    echo  program ( "PHP" ); // Value for the first parameter
```

Result with predetermined parameters:

Know how to program with HTML and PHP .

```
// Default Parameters
function default ( $ dis = "design" ) {



    return "How to make a $ dis .";



}



    default echo (); // Pick up the

    default echo  parameter value (null); // Do not pick up anything
by default ("program"); // Collect the calling value
```

How to make a design. -> Without parameters

How to do an . -> NULL parameter

How to make a program . -> Value as parameter

```php
// Default parameters
// Use of arrays and special type NULL as default defaults
function predetArray ( $ code = array ( "HTML" ), $ programming =
NULL) {


    // If there are no parameters ( NULL ) in the call , then it returns
'NotePat ++'

    $ manager = is_null ( $ programming ) ? "NotePat ++": $
programming;



    // Return parameters separated by a comma ( , ) plus the value
of the variable ' $ manager '

    return "Schedule a web". join (",", $ code). "using $ manager.

    <br /> ";
```

}

//

Caller code echo predetArray () ;

echo   predetArray (array ("HTML", "PHP"), "Dreamweaver CS6");

Call without parameters:

Program an HTML web using NotePat ++ .

Call with parameters:

Program HTML, PHP web using Dreamweaver CS6 .

Go up

Variable length parameter lists

PHP contains support for variable-length parameter lists in user-defined functions. PHP contains the following functions to support these features.

func_num_args () : Returns the number of parameters passed the roles.

func_get_arg (num): (num) from a list of parameters.

21

func_get_args () : Returns an array formed by a list of function parameters.

NOTE: These functions can be used within a function.

func_num_args () Returns the number of parameters passed in the function

```php
// func_num_args ()

function numParam () {


    // Number of arguments for the function

    $ numArgs = func_num_args ();

    echo  "Number of past parameters: $ numArgs  <br />"; // Return 4


}


// Call function with 4 parameters

numParam ( 4, 14, 24, 34 );
```

func_num_args () Number of parameters of the numParam function : 4

Go up

func_get_arg (num) Returns an element of the parameters of the function.

```php
// func_get_arg (num)

function collectsParam () {


    // Number of arguments for the function

    $ numArgs = func_num_args ();


    echo  "Number of parameters of the numParam function : $ numArgs <br />";


        if ($ numArgs> = 3) {


        // Generates a warning if we indicate a number

        // of parameters greater than the number of

        // parameters passed currently

        echo "The third parameter is the number:". func_get_arg ( 2 ) . "<br />";
```

```
    }

}
```

// Call function with 4 parameters

pickParam (4, 14, 24, 34);

func_get_arg (num) Number of parameters of the numParam function : 4 The third parameter is the number: 24

The func_get_arg () function can be used together with the function func_get_args () and func_num_args () , this will allow user functions to accept lists of variable length parameters.

Go up

func_get_args () Returns matrix with the parameters of the function.

// func_get_args ()

echo " func_get_args ()

";

function collectsParam2 () {

```php
// Number of arguments of the function

$ numArgs = func_num_args ();

echo " Number of parameters of the numParam function : $ numArgs <br />";


    if ($ numArgs> = 3) {

    // Generates a warning if we indicate a number

    // of parameters greater than the number of

    // past parameters currently

    echo " The fourth parameter is the number: ". func_get_arg ( 3 ) "<br />";


    }



// We return the array of the parameters of the function

$ listParam = func_get_args ();



// ' array_sum () ' returns the sum of all the values of an

echo array " We add the parameters: ". array_sum ( $ listParam ). "<br />";
```

```
for ( $ x = 0; $ x <$ numArgs; $ x ++ ) {


    echo " The argument $ x is: ". $ listParam [ $ x ]. "<br />";


}

}
```

// Call function with 4 parameters

pickParam (4, 14, 24, 34);

func_get_args () Number of parameters of the numParam function: 4 The fourth parameter is the number: 34 We add the parameters: 76 Array of the parameters of the function: Parameter 0 is the: 4 Parameter 1 is the: 14 Parameter 2 is the: 24 Parameter 3 is: 34

Go up

Return of values (functions)

When we want to return a value, we will use the return statement. This statement can only return a value, but it can be a simple value or include arrays and objects. This causes the function to finish its execution immediately and pass control back to the line from which it was called. The return variable can also be a reference to a variable using the ampersand operator (&).

Array as a return value

```php
// Return values of a function as an Array

function returnArray () {


    $ arr = array ( 10, 'twenty', 30 );

    return  $ arr ; // Return the array value


}


    // Declare variable to store values of type Array

    $ verArray = array ();


    // Pass the returned values of the function to the variable

    $ verArray = returnArray () ;


    //

    Go through the foreach values ( $ verArray as $ cla => $ val ) {
```

```
    echo $ val ;



  }
```

Array as a return value Index 0 /> 10 Index 1 /> twenty Index 2 />
30

Return of values

```
// Return a list of values

function iva ( $ base , $ porcen = 21 ) {


  return $ base * $ percentage / 100 ;


}


  // Multiple calls to a function
```

// Calculate the base by the 2 or parameter of the function ' $ porcen = 21 '

echo iva (100). "<br />"; // Returns 21

// Calculates the base by '8' thus changing the value of the 2 or parameter of the function

echo iva (100, 8). "<br />"; // Returns 8

// Calculates the base by '0' thus changing the value of the 2 or parameter of the function

echo iva (100, 0). "<br />"; // Return 0

Return of values 21% of 100:> 21 8% of 100:> 8 0% of 100:> 0

Returning a reference from a function

We can return a reference to a variable, and not a copy so that the function can modify the variable. We will use the ampersand symbol as a reference indicator, which will be placed in the definition of the function "before the name of the function" and in the assignment in the function call.

// Return a reference from a

class object function {

public $ unvalor = 100 ;

```
public function & obtainValue () {

    return $ this -> val ;

}

}
```

$ obj = new object ;

$ elvalor = & $ obj -> getValue (); // '$ elvalor' is a reference to '$ obj -> val', which is 100 .

$ obj -> val = 20 ;

echo $ thevalor; // Returns the new value of '$ obj -> val', that is, 20 .

New value of the variable: 20

Go up

Variable functions

These variable functions will allow us to implement function call tables and return calls "callback functions."

The way PHP works with these functions is when it encounters a variable followed by parentheses " ()," it will search if there exists a function with the same name of the variable, executing it if it finds it.

```php
// Variable functions


// Function variable

function function () {


    echo " 1 er Text from a function. <br />";

}


// Function variable

function func_2 () {


    echo " 2 or Text from another function. <br />";



}



// function concatenated variable

function funcion_4 () {


    echo " 3 er Text from a function created from two concatenated
texts. <br />";
```

}

// Calls to variable functions

$ mifuncion = " function "; // Assign string to variable

$ myfunction (); // Call the function by the name of the assigned string

$ mifuncion = " func_2 "; // Assign string to variable

$ myfunction (); // the roles to it's string

// Concatenate values of two variables to form a new ' variable function '

$ annex = " _4 ";

$ mifuncion = " function ". $ annex ; // Return 'funcion_4 '

$ mifuncion () ; // Call function ' funcion_4 () ' through the concatenation of two texts

1 er Text from a function.

2 o Text from another function.

3 er Text from a function created from two concatenated texts.

Object methods can also be described with the variable function syntax.

```
// Variable method

class  Object {


    // Function called from outside the class

    function Variable () {


        $ nom = 'Other'; // We assign ' Other ' to variable ' $ nom '

        $ this -> $ nom (); // Call the function ' Other () ' within this
same class


    }


    // Function called from within the same class

    function Other () {


        // Message that will show on the screen
```

echo " We are in the function ' Other () ' that has been called from another function,

within the same class. ";

}

}

$ myObject = new Object () ;

$ nomFun = " Variable "; // We assign ' Variable ' to variable ' $ nomFun '

$ myObject -> $ nomFun () ; // Call the function ' Variable () ' inside class ' Object '

The methods of objects

We are in the ' Other () ' function that has been called from another function, within the same class.

NOTE: With these constructions of the language we cannot use the variable functions:

echo (), print (), unset (), isset (), empty (), include (), require (), etc
...

These language constructions we should not confuse them with functions.

Very important is that the variables must have an assigned value, since otherwise, we will get an error message (indefinite function).

Go up

Recursivity between functions

The recursion in a function, is the ability of these to call themselves, facilitating and much coding, especially in calculations and mathematical problems. A recursive function is called itself until a condition is met, for example, we are going to calculate the factorial of a number.

Calculation of the factorial of a whole number

```
// Recursivity of the functions

// Calculate the factorial of 4

$ integer = 4;


// Function call with
```

```php
echo parameter "<br /> Factorial of". $ whole. " is " . (factorial ($
integer) );


function factorial ($ factorial) {


    // Recursive call to factorial ()

    // $ var , local variable of each factorial function

    if ($ factorial == 0)


    // Return ' 1 ', which will multiply it by

    // resulting number and the function will end.

    return 1;

    echo " Multiply by". $ factorial . "<br />";

     // Function calls back to itself

    // Subtract ' -1 ' to go down to the number ' 1 ' end

    return $ factorial *  factorial ($ factorial -1 ) ;


}

Multiply by 4

Multiply by 3
```

Multiply by 2

Multiply by 1

Factorial of 4 is 24

Recursion of a function


```php
// Recursivity of functions

function otherRecursive ( $ time ) {


    // If parameter is equal to ' 4 ' ...

    if ( $ time == 4 ):


        echo " Last time: 4 round <br />";

        // While parameter is not equal to '4' ...

    else:


        echo " Vez number:". $ time . "<br />";


        // And it calls itself
```

```
        anotherRecursive ( $ time  +  1 );


    endif;



}
```

```
        // Calling the function with recursion

        // Pass parameter ' 1 ' indicating that the start

        // the account starts from ' 1 '.

        otherRecursive ( 1 );
```

Recursion function

Time number: 1 to

Time number: 2 to

Time number: 3 to

Time: 4 to return

Go up

Scope of the variables

It is the context in which you can access a variable: global and local.

LOCAL: It is by default when a variable is defined within a function. That is, it is not accessible from outside the function.

GLOBAL: It is the one that is defined outside the functions, and we can use them within the functions. PHP forces us to define explicitly within the function, global variables to be able to use them within the $ CLOBALS matrix function.

$ CLOBALS: If we want to avoid the global definition, we can use the associative matrix that all the global variables have. $ CLOBALS is one superglobal.

SUPERGLOBAL: It is a set of variables that are globales automatically; it is not necessary to define them as global within a function.

The global definition of a variable

// We define a global variable

$ varGlobal = 20; // global variable

// Ways to access global variables

```
function TestSinGlobal () {

  $ varGlobal ++ ; // local variable (THIS LINE CAN SHOW AN ERROR)

  echo "Test without global . $ varGlobal: ". $ varGlobal. "in

      the absence of a global definition and not using $ GLOBALS,

          it is treated as a local variable. ";


  // As there is no global definition and do not use

  // $ GLOBALS, $ varGlobal is treated as a local variable

  // for that reason, print 1 instead of 21.

}


  // Call function

  TestSinGlobal () ;
```

Variable without global definition .

Test without global. $ varGlobal: 1 as there is no global definition and you do not use $ GLOBALS, it is treated as a local variable.

```
// Variable defined as' global ' within function
```

$ varGlobal = 20; // global variable

// Ways to access global variables

function TestConGlobal () {

   global 20 ; // Global definition

  $ varGlobal ++;

  echo "Test with global . $ varGlobal   :". $ varGlobal . "It is

      no longer local, it is treated as global. ";

  // 20 is no longer local, it is treated as global

  // print 21

}

  // Call function

  TestConGlobal () ;

Variable defined as' global '.

Try with global. $ varGlobal: 21 is no longer local; it is treated as global.

```php
// Variable defined as ' $ GLOBALS ' inside function

$ varGlobal = 20; // global variable


// Ways to access global variables

function TestConGlobals () {

    $ GLOBALS [" varGlobal "] ++; // Definition global

    echo "Try with $ GLOBALS . $ VarGlobal   : ". $ GLOBALS
["varGlobal"]. "It

        is not local anymore; it is globally common. ";


    // $ varGlobal is no longer local, it is a global common

    // print 22

}


    // Call function

    TestConGlobals () ;

Variable defined as ' $ GLOBALS '.
```

Try with $ GLOBALS. $ varGlobal: 22 is no longer local; it is treated as global.

Go up

Date and time functions

Through the function time () we will control the passage of time such as: activate a process at a certain time, print the date and time, find out differences between two values of date and time, etc ... This date and time value is a numeric value that indicates the time in seconds elapsed since (1/1/1970).

Some systems can obtain this value in microseconds using the microtime () function.

These functions can be classified into types: They return the value of date or time.

They edit the date and time value based on the pre-determined format.

Validate the dates.

Table of date and time functions

Table of date and time functions

FUNCTION   DESCRIPTION Go up

Characters for the 'format' parameter of the date (format) function

Characters for the 'format' parameter of the date (format) function

CHARACTER   DESCRIPTION   RETURNED VALUESGo up

getdate (): Returns an associative array with the detailed and disaggregated information of the date and time.

// Complete date and time information

$ inforFechaHora = getdate () ;

   var_dump ($ inforFechaHora);

Seconds /> 54

Minutes /> 15

Hours /> 20

Day /> 20

Number of the day of the week /> 4 = Thursday

Number of the month /> 6

Year /> 2019

Number of the day of the year /> 170

Name of the day of the week /> Thursday

Name of the month /> June

Seconds since 1/1/1970 /> 1561061754

WHAT CAN PHP DO?

Anything. PHP is mainly focused on programming server-side scripts, so you can do anything that another CGI program can do, such as accumulating form data, generating pages with dynamic content, or sending and receiving cookies although PHP can do much more.

There are mainly three main fields where PHP scripts are used.

1. **Server-side scripts.** This is the most traditional field and the main focus. Three things are necessary for this to work: the PHP analyzer (CGI module or server), a web server and a web browser. It is important to run the server with a connected PHP installation. You can access the result of the PHP program with a browser, viewing the PHP page through the server. All this can be run on your machine if you are experienced with PHP programming. See the section on installation instructions for more information.

2. **Scripts from the command line.** You can create a PHP script and run it without the need of a server or browser. Only the PHP parser is needed to use it in this way. This kind of use is ideal for scripts that run regularly using cron (in * nix or Linux) or the Task Scheduler (in Windows). These scripts can also be utilized for simple text processing tasks. See the section Using PHP in the command line for more information.

3. **Write desktop applications.** Probably PHP is not the most appropriate language to create desktop applications with a

graphical user interface, but if you know PHP well, and would like to use some advanced PHP features in client-side applications, you can use PHP-GTK to write such programs. It is also possible to write independent applications of a platform in this way. PHP-GTK is an extension of PHP, not available in the main distribution. If you are interested in PHP-GTK, you can visit your website.

PHP can be used in all major operating systems, including Linux, many variants of Unix (including HP-UX, Solaris, and OpenBSD), macOS, RISC OS, Microsoft Windows, and others. PHP supports most of today's web servers, including Apache, IIS, and many others. This includes any web server that can use the PHP FastCGI binary, such as Lighttpd and Nginx. PHP works both as a module and a CGI processor.

So with PHP, you have the freedom to choose the operating system and the web server. Also, you can use programming by procedures or object-oriented programming (OOP), or a mixture of both.

With PHP, you are not limited to generating HTML. The capabilities of PHP include the creation of images, PDF files, and even Flash movies (using libswf and Ming) generated on the fly. You can also easily generate any type of text, such as XHTML and any other type of XML file. PHP can autogenerate these files and keep them in the file system instead of printing them on the screen, creating a cache on the server side for dynamic content.

One of the most powerful and remarkable features of PHP is its support for a wide range of databases. Writing a web page with access to a database is incredibly simple using one of the database-specific extensions (e.g., for mysql), or using an abstraction layer as a PDO , or connecting to any database that supports the standard of Open Connection to Databases through the ODBC extension. Other databases could use cURL or sockets, as CouchDB does.

PHP also has support to communicate with other services using protocols such as LDAP, IMAP, SNMP, NNTP, POP3, HTTP, COM (in Windows) and many others. You can also create pure network sockets and interact using any other protocol. PHP has support for the exchange of complex WDDX data between virtually all web programming languages. And speaking of interconnection, PHP has support for the installation of Java objects and use them transparently as PHP objects.

PHP has useful text processing highlights, which include regular expressions compatible with Perl (PCRE), and many extensions and tools for accessing and analyzing XML documents. PHP standardizes all XML extensions on the solid foundation of libxml2, and extends this feature set by adding support for SimpleXML, XMLReader and XMLWriter.

There are other interesting extensions, which are categorized alphabetically and by category. There are also additional extensions of PECL that could be documented or not within the PHP manual, such as XDebug.

Part 1

PHP AND PROGRAMMING OF FUNCTIONS

Before starting, we must be clear about what a function is. This class of structures is based on a premise: they receive a parameter and return a result. However, this is not invariably the case, since they can receive several parameters, or not return any, but it is not the case of those that we are going to deal with today. This is important because we must remember that in programming, not only do we have the functions that give us predefined languages, but we can also build our custom functions to work with and treat the code and user interactions. We see a function written such that:

Function (parameters) {

Body

Return of value

}

We must translate this structure to the target language, of course, since functions are not written in the same way in Java as in C ++.

Now that we understand what a function is let's see a few related to PHP that will certainly be useful in any field because they are quite generic. Let us begin.

49

Empty (). This function is responsible for checking if a variable is empty. Look at how it is written. We have the name of the function and a parenthesis. We are going to put inside that parenthesis the variable that we want to check if it is empty since it is the parameter that we are going to pass to the function, which returns a Boolean value, that is, true or false. This can be used to verify states and thus avoid errors in the loading of the code. Remember that PHP is not too strict and when you encounter this kind of problem, the whole infrastructure is resented, so I recommend you do this kind of checks.

Echo (). This is the equivalent of "print" in JavaScript. It simply shows on screen the parameter that we are passing, whether the content of a variable, a text string, etc. Very important also to show some data quickly and without complicating too much in the procedure.

Count () . Very important, too, the count is responsible for counting (as indicated by its name) the number of elements that have a list of objects, for example, an array or matrix. This is very useful when we want to relate a loop to the number of elements in an array. For example, imagine that we want to generate a table by screen, which will grow or decrease depending on the contents of an array. With count (), we will know how many laps the loop that builds the table should give, without having to juggle more.

Die (). How dramatic! But do not fear, this function is responsible for "kill" the execution of the current script. Why? Every time a script finishes its operations, it is better that we kill it to stop consuming resources on the server. The most classic example is a connection to a database: it is an operation that consumes browser, server and database resources, be it Oracle or SQL. We do not want this situation since the result is slower navigation for the client and an overload in the server. Solution? We execute the Die () function when everything is finished, and thus we make sure that we do not have scripts running in the background without our noticing.

Ceil () and Floor (). Two of the mathematical functions that you are going to use the most. They are responsible, respectively, for rounding up, with ceil (ceiling), or down, with the floor (floor), a value with decimals. Sometimes we will want to count the numerical values as integers, instead of floating, and with these two functions, we have what we need to be able to transform these values without complicating our lives.

As said earlier, these functions are, its universal, in the sense that all programming languages have **equivalence**, except Die, so be encourage you to look for their homonym in JavaScript, for example.

WHAT DO I NEED?

In this manual, it is assumed that there is a server that has PHP support enabled and that PHP handles all files with the extension .php. On maximum servers, this is the default extension for PHP files, although you can ask the administrator of your server to be sure. If the server has support for PHP, then it is not necessary to do anything. Simply create your .php files, save them in your web directory and the server will analyze them for you. There is no necessity to compile anything or install other tools. Think of these files enabled for PHP as simple HTML files with the addition of a new family of magic labels that allow all kinds of things.

Let's say you want to save the precious bandwidth and work locally. In this case, you will want to install a web server, such as Apache, and of course, PHP. The safest thing is that you also want to install a database like MySQL.

You can install them independently, or you can choose a simpler way. This manual contains PHP Installation Instructions (assuming you have some type of web server already configured). If you have problems with the installation, we suggest that you ask your questions on our »installation mailing list. If you choose the simplest way, locate a preconfigured package for your operating system, which automatically installs all of this with just a few mouse clicks. It is easy to configure a web server with support for PHP in any operating system, including MacOSX, Linux, and Windows. On Linux, you might find useful rpmfind, and PBoneto locates the RPM. You can also visit apt-get to find packages for Debian.

HYPERTEXT MARKING LANGUAGE

Html (Hypertext Markup Language). Use marks to describe how text and graphics should appear in a Web Browser that, in turn, are ready to read those marks and display the information in a standard format. Some Web browsers include additional tags that can only be read and used by them, and not by other browsers. The use of non-standard marks in places of special importance is not recommended.

The beginning

Html started as a simplification of something called SGML, Generalized Standard Markup Language, much more difficult to learn than HTML and generally used to show large amounts of data that must be published in different ways. The theory says that all brands are not just a format code for the text, but have a meaning of their own. Therefore, everything that can be used must be within a brand with meaning. To "read" an HTML page without a Web browser you should be familiar with some terms and concepts. The first one is the source or source code, the way to name all the marks and the text that make up the HTML file. The source is what you will see when you use a text editor, and not a Web browser, to view the HTML file.

A brand is the basic element of the code that assigns the format to the page and tells the browser how to display certain elements. Brands do not appear when Web Pages are displayed, but they are a fundamental part of HTML creation. These symbols are essential; they will tell the browser that it is an instruction, not the text that should appear on the screen.

Many brands need what is called the final brand. It is usually the same brand, but putting a backslash to its meaning. For example, the mark for the letter in Bold is <B> and must be placed before the text on which it should take effect, putting the closing mark </B> behind it. If it is not closed, there will never be parts of the document that are not displayed correctly or, what is worse, an error will occur in the browser due to incorrect syntax.

An attribute appears directly within a mark, between the <> symbols. It modifies certain aspects of the brand and tells the browser to show the information with additional special characteristics. Although the mark to use an image is <IMG>, they have a necessary attribute, SRC, which tells the browser where the graphic file can be found. It also has several optional attributes such as HEIGHT, WIDTH, and ALIGN.

Most of the attributes are optional and allow you to skip the default values of the browser and customize the appearance of certain elements.

Whenever a mark appears with a backslash, like </ B> or </ HTML> it will be "closing" or ending the mark of that section. Not all brands have a closing mark (such as the image mark), and some of them are optional (such as <IP>).

An attribute usually has a value; expressed with the sign of equal (=). If you use attributes with values, they are always put in quotation marks, unless they are numbers that do not need them (although it is a good habit).

The browsers are responsible for interpreting the HTML code of the documents, and for showing users the web pages resulting from the interpreted code.

Versions

In November of 1995, the HTML 2.0 standard was approved. For the creation of web pages. It was created with informative objectives, oriented to the academic activity, in which the content of the pages held more valuable than the design.

Although this version of HTML lacked several tools to control the design of the pages and add multimedia content, so Netscape (whose browsers were the most used in the years) began to incorporate new labels that did not exist in the standard.

The committee in charge of establishing the standards within the Internet began to work on the plan of a new version of HTML, the draft of HTML 3.0.

But this draft was too extensive, trying to include numerous new attributes for existing labels and the creation of many other new labels. Therefore, it was not well received by the market, and several companies joined to form a new committee in charge of establishing the HTML standards. This committee was renamed W3C.

In January 1997, the HTML 3.2 standard was approved. This new standard included the improvements provided by the Internet Explorer and Netscape Navigator browsers, which had already made extensions to the HTML 2.0 standard.

In December 1997, the HTML 4.0 standard was approved, created to standardize frames, style sheets, and scripts.

In September of 2001, the HTML 4.01 standard was approved.

HTML 5

HTML 5 consists of many different modules, whose degree of the specification is at disparate levels. Therefore, many of the features of HTML 5 are ready to be implemented, at a point of development that is close to the one that will finally be presented. Many other features are still simply in the pipeline, by way of initial ideas or drafts.

The newer versions of almost all browsers, including the controversial Internet Explorer 8, implement some of the features of HTML 5 '. Of course, for a website to look good in all systems, we must use only those parts that work in all browsers, so today, few are really available utilities of the language, if we want to make a site compatible web, However, in the worst case, we can begin to use these features at an experimental level, if only to rub our hands waiting to really incorporate them into our usual development practices.

What's new in HTML 5

HTML 5 includes significant news in various fields. It is not only about incorporating new labels or eliminating others, but it means improvements in areas that up to now were outside the language and for which other technologies needed to be used.

Body structure: Most webs hold a common format, consisting of elements like the header, footer, browsers, etc. HTML 5 lets you group all these parts of a web into new labels that will serve each of the typical parts of a page.

Tags for specific content: Until now a single tag was used to incorporate various types of rich content, such as Flash or video animations. Now specific labels will be used for each type of content in particular, such as audio, video, etc.

Canvas: is a new element that will allow drawing, through the functions of an API, on the page, all kinds of forms, which may be animated and reply to user intercommunication. It is something similar to the possibilities offered by Flash, but within the HTML specification and without the need to have any plugin installed.

Local databases: the browser will support the use of a local database, with which you can work on a web page through the client and an API. It is something like Cookies but designed to store large amounts of information, which will allow the creation of web applications that work without having to be connected to the Internet.

Web Workers: these are processes that require a lot of processing time by the browser, but they can be done in the background so that the user does not have to wait for them to finish starting using the page. This will also have an API for working with Web Workers.

Offline web applications: There will be another API for working with web applications, which can be developed so that they also work locally and without being connected to the Internet.

Geolocation: Web pages can be located geographically using an API that allows Geolocation.

New APIs for the user interface: topics as used as "drag & drop" (drag and drop) in the user interfaces of conventional programs, will be incorporated into HTML 5 through an API.

End of the presentation labels: all the labels that have to do with the presentation of the document, that is, that modify styles of the page, will be eliminated. The responsibility for defining the appearance of a website will be borne solely by CSS.

Browsers, compatibility

As we said, the browser installed on the user's computer is the one that interprets the HTML code of the page you visit, so sometimes it can happen that two users view the same page differently because they have different browsers installed or even different versions. From the same browser.

Today's browsers claim to be compatible with the latest version of HTML. It is necessary to make extensions of the browsers so that they can be compatible with this latest version.

Two of the browsers that are continuously making extensions are Internet Explorer and Netscape Navigator, which perform extensions even before the standards are established, trying to include the new functions included in the drafts.

Browsers must be compatible with the latest HTML version to interpret as many labels as possible. If a browser does not recognize a tag, it ignores it, and the effect that the tag intended is not reflected on the page.

To make the extensions of these browsers, new attributes are added to existing tags, or new tags are added.

As a result of these extensions, there will be pages whose code can be interpreted completely by all browsers, while others, by including new attributes or draft tags of the latest version of HTML, can only be interpreted in their entirety in the most updated browsers.

In the latter case it can also happen that some page tag can only be interpreted by a specific browser and another tag by a browser different from the previous one, so it would never be viewed in its entirety by any browser.

One of the challenges for web designers is to make the pages more attractive using the full power of the HTML language but taking into account these compatibility problems so that the greatest number of Internet users see their pages as they have been designed.

Editors

An editor is a program that allows us to write documents. Today there are a large number of editors that allow you to create web pages without the need to write a particular line of code [[HTML]. These editors have a visual environment, and automatically generate the code of the pages. By being able to see at all times how the page will be in the browser, the creation of the pages is facilitated, and the use of menus allows gaining speed.

These visual editors can sometimes generate junk code, i.e., code that is useless, at other times it may be more effective to directly correct the code, so it is necessary to know HTML to debug the code of the pages.

Some of the visual editors with which you can create your web pages are Macromedia Dreamweaver, Microsoft Frontpage, Adobe Pagemill, NetObjects Fusion, CutePage, HotDog Professional, Netscape Composer and Arachnophilia, some of which have the advantage of being free.

In aulaClic, you can find the courses of Macromedia Dreamweaver and Microsoft Frontpage, two of the most used editors today.

It is advisable to start using a tool as simple as possible, to have to insert the HTML code ourselves. This allows you to become intimate with the language, to be able to use a visual editor later and to debug the code when necessary.

To create web pages by writing the HTML code directly, you can use any plain text editor so as Wordpad or Notepad in Windows, or powerful Vim or Emacs editors in Unix and GNU / Linux environments.

Labels

Labels or marks delimit each of the elements that make up an HTML document. There are two types of labels, the element start, and end or end element.

The start tag is delimited by the characters <and>. It is composed of the identifier or name of the tag and may contain a series of optional attributes that allow certain properties to be added. Its syntax is: <identifier attribute1 attribute2 ...>

The attributes of the start tag follow a predefined syntax and can take any user-specific value, or predefined HTML values.

The end tag is delimited by the characters </ and>. It is composed of the identifier or name of the tag and does not contain attributes. Its syntax is: </ identifier>

Each of the elements of the page will be found between a start tag and its corresponding closing tag, except some elements that do not need a closing tag. It is also possible to nest tags, that is, insert tags between other start and end tags.

It is important to nest the labels well, the labels cannot be 'crossed', in the example we start with the label <p ..>, before closing this label we have put the <font ..> so before closing the label <p ..> we must close the tag label <font ..>.

YOUR FIRST PAGE WITH PHP

Start by creating a file called hello.php and put it in the root directory of your web server (DOCUMENT_ROOT) including the following content:

For instance# 1 Our first PHP script: hello.php

```
<html>

<head>

 <title>Prueba de PHP</title>

</head>

<body>

<?php echo '<p>Hola Mundo</p>'; ?>

</body>

</html>
```

Use your web browser to access the file with the URL of your server, finalized with the reference to the /hola.php file. If you are programming locally, this URL will be something like http://localhost/hola.php or http://127.0.0.1/hola.php, but this depends on the configuration of your web server. If everything is configured correctly, the file will be analyzed by PHP and the following content will be sent to your browser:

```
<html>

<head>

<title> PHP Test </ title>

</ head>

<body>

<p> Hello world </ p>

</ body>

</ html>
```

This program is extremely simple and it really is not necessary to use PHP to create a page like this one. The only thing that shows is: Hello world using the sentence echo of PHP. Note that the file does not require being executable or special in any way. The server recognizes that this file needs to be interpreted by PHP due to the use of the extension ".php", since the server is configured to send it to PHP. Think as if it were a normal HTML file that has a series of special tags available with which you can do many interesting things.

If you tried to use this example and did not produce any results, you were asked if you wanted to download the file, or the whole file was shown as text, most likely PHP is not enabled on your server or is not configured correctly. Ask your administrator to enable it using the Installation chapter of the manual. If you are working locally, also read the chapter dedicated to the installation to make sure everything is configured correctly. Make sure you are accessing the file via HTTP and that the server shows the result. If you are opening the file from the file system, it probably will not be analyzed by PHP. If the difficulty continues, do not hesitate to use any of the multiple options of the Support for PHP.

The objective of this example is the format of the PHP special tags. In this example, we use <? Php to show the start of a PHP tag. Then we put the sentence and leave PHP mode adding the closing tag ?>. In this way, you can enter and exit PHP mode in an HTML file whenever you want. For more information, read the section of the manual entitled Basic PHP Syntax.

Note: An observation about line advances

- Line feeds make little sense in HTML, although it's still a good idea to make the HTML code look clean and clear by putting line feeds. PHP will automatically remove line feeds that are after a closing tag ?>. This can be very useful when putting many PHP blocks or including files that contain PHP and that are supposed to show nothing. At the very time, it can be a bit complicated. You can place a space after the closing tag ?> To forcefully display space and a line feed, or you can put an explicit line feed in the last echo/print within the PHP block.

Note: An observation about text editors

There are several text editors and Integrated Development Environments (IDE) that can be used to create, edit, and manage

PHP files. You can find a partial list of these in List of PHP editors. If you want to recommend an editor, please visit the page mentioned above and ask the maintainer of the page to include it in the list. Having an editor that highlights the syntax can be very helpful.

Note: An observation about the word processors

Text processors such as StarOffice Writer, Microsoft Word and Abiword are not good options for editing PHP files. If you need to practice one of these programs to test this script, be sure to save the document as plain text, or else PHP will not be able to read it and execute it.

Note: An observation about Windows Notepad

If you write your PHP scripts using the Windows Notepad, you should make sure that your files are saved with the extension .php. (Notepad automatically adds the .txt extension to the files unless you follow the next steps to prevent it.) When you save the file, and the program asks you what name you want to give the file, enclose the name (that is, " hello.php "). An alternative is to click on the "Text Documents (* .txt)" drop-down menu in the "Save as" dialog box, and change to the "All files (*. *)" Option. Here you can type the name of the file without the quotes.

Now that you have created a small PHP script that works correctly, it's time to design the most famous PHP script: get a call to the phpinfo () function to get a lot of useful information about your system and configuration, such as the predefined variables available, PHP modules loaded, and configuration settings . Take some time to review this valuable erudition.

Example # 2 Obtain system information from PHP

```
<?php phpinfo(); ?>
```

DEAL WITH FORMS

Another of the most powerful features of PHP is how to manage HTML forms. The fundamental concept that is important to understand is that any element of a form will be automatically available in your PHP scripts. Please read the segment of the manual on Variables from external sources for more information and examples on how to use forms with PHP. Let's look at an example:

Example # 1 A simple HTML form

```
<form action = "accion.php" method = "post">

<p> Your full name: <input type = "text" full name = "name" /> </
p>

<p> Your age: <input type = "text" full name = "age" /> </ p>

<p> <input type = "submit" /> </ p>

</ form>
```

There is nothing special in this form. It's just an HTML form without any special tag class. When the user completes this form and presses the send button, the page accion.php is called. In this file you could write something like this:

Example # 2 Show information of our form

```
Hola <?php echo htmlspecialchars($_POST['nombre']); ?>.
```

Usted tiene <?php echo (int)$_POST['edad']; ?> años.

An example of the result of this script could be:

Hello Jose. You are 22 years old.

Except for the parts of htmlspecialchars () and (int), it should be obvious what the code does. htmlspecialchars () ensures that any character that is special in HTML is properly encoded so that no one can inject HTML or Javascript tags into the page. The age field, considering we know it is a number, we can convert it to an integer value that will automatically get rid of any non-numeric character. You can also do the same with PHP with the filter extension. The variables $ _POST ['name'] and $ _POST ['age'] they are automatically set by PHP. Previously we used the superglobal $ _SERVER; above we introduced the superglobal $ _POST, which contains all the POST data. Note that the method of our form is POST. If we had used the GET method, our information would be in place in the superglobal $ _GET. You could also use the $ _REQUEST superglobal if you do not care about the source of the requested data. It contains all the information about the data of getting, POST, and COOKIE mixed.

In PHP, you can also deal with XForms entries; although you probably feel comfortable with the HTML forms at first, which are widely supported. Although working with XForms is not for beginners, they might be of interest to you. If so, in the features section, there is a short introduction to the manipulation of data received from XForms.

USE THE OLD CODE IN NEW VERSIONS OF PHP

Now that PHP has grown and has become a popular language, many more repositories and libraries contain code that you can reuse. The PHP developers have tried to preserve the backward compatibility, that is, if a script were written for an old version, it would work (ideally) without any change in a recent version of PHP. In practice, some changes are usually necessary.

Two of the most important changes that affect the old code are:

The old $ HTTP _ * _ VARS arrays are no longer available as of PHP 5.4.0. The following superglobal designs were presented in PHP 4.1.0. They are: $ _GET , $ _POST , $ _COOKIE , $ _SERVER , $ _FILES , $ _ENV , $ _REQUEST , and $ _SESSION .

External variables last no longer registered in the global scope by default. In other words, as of PHP 4.2.0, the PHP directive register_globals is disabled (off) by default in php.ini. The best method to access these values is by using the superglobal variables mentioned above. The scripts, books, and old tutorials could count on this directive being activated (on). If it were on, for example, $ id could be used from the URL http://www.example.com/foo.php?id=42. Whether it is activated or deactivated,$ _GET ['id'] is always available.

GENERAL INSTALLATION CONSIDERATIONS

Before you start with the installation, you first need to know what you want to use PHP for. There are three main fields where you can use PHP as described in the section: What can be done with PHP?

Web applications and websites (server-side scripting)

Scripting on the command line

Desktop applications (GUI)

For the first-mentioned form, which is the most common, you need three things: PHP, a web server and a web browser. Surely you already have the web browser and, depending on the configuration of the operating system, you may already have a web server (e.g., Apache in Linux and macOS, IIS in Windows). You can also rent web space in a company. In this way, you do not need to install anything, just write the PHP scripts, upload them to the server you rent and see the results in your browser.

If you configure the server and PHP on your own, there are two options for how to connect PHP to the server. For many servers, PHP has a direct interface module (also named SAPI). These servers comprise Apache, Microsoft Internet Information Server, Netscape, and iPlanet. Many other servers have aid for ISAPI, the Microsoft interface module (OmniHTTPd for example). If PHP does not support your web server module, you can always use it as a CGI or FastCGI processor. This means configuring the server to use the PHP executable CGI to process each of the requests to PHP files on the server.

If you are also excited in using PHP under the command line (e.g., write scripts that autogenerate images offline, or process text files depending on the arguments that are passed to them), you will always need the command line executable. For more information, read the section on writing PHP applications from the command line. In this case, no server or browser is needed.

With PHP you can additionally write desktop GUI applications using the PHP-GTK extension. This approach has nothing to do with writing web pages since nothing of HTML is shown, but it manages windows and objects inside them. For more information about PHP-GTK, please hit the site assigned to this extension. PHP-GTK is not involved in the official PHP distribution.

From here on, this section deals with the configuration of PHP for web servers on Unix and Windows, including server module interfaces and CGI executables. You can also find information about command line executables in the following sections.

PHP source code and binary orders for Windows can be found at https://www.php.net/downloads.php. It is recommended choosing a nearby alternative site to download the distributions

.

Part 2

STYLE GUIDE FOR PHP

A style guide to a programming language is a set of recommendations on how to format programs. The interest in using a specific style is to facilitate code reuse and error detection. There are many styles of programming, and you cannot say that one is better than another, but it is convenient to adopt a certain style and use it consistently.

The style used in these notes and which is recommended by the students is based on:

First, in the PSR-1 and PSR-2 style guides of the PHP-FIG group (PHP Framework Interop Group), a group in which the authors of the most popular PHP frameworks participate,

Secondly, in the official style guide of the PEAR project, the old library repository for PHP that since around 2015 can be considered obsolete (and has been replaced by Composer as a package distribution tool).

Note: In December 2018, PEAR suffered a security breach that was not discovered until January 2019 [reference], which led to the immediate closure of the PEAR server, although it was reopened in February 2019.

Third, in the personal preferences of the author.

Note: There is an official PHP style guide, but this guide refers to the PHP source code, which is written in C, and is intended for programmers who develop the language, it does not refer to programs written in PHP.

In this lesson, the most important style recommendations are discussed. When the style rules...

Come from PSR-1, PSR-2 and PEAR, style rules use the expressions "must ..." or "should not ...".

Come from PSR-1, PSR-2 or PEAR, the name of the guide is indicated in brackets.

The teachers' choices have used the expressions "it is advised ..." or "it is not necessary ...".

The Eclipse for PHP developers configuration lesson explains how to configure Eclipse PHP to format a program according to the PSR-2 style recommendations.

Recommended style guide for students

File formats

[PSR-1] Files must be saved in UTF-8 format without BOM.

[PSR-2] Files must use the Unix format (LF character as the end of the line and at the end of the last line of the file).

Php configuration

[PEAR] The code should not generate errors or warnings when the error_reporting directive has the value E_STRICT.

PHP block delimiters

PHP fragments should be delimited with <? Php ...?> And not with <? ...?> .

<?php

print "<p>Hola</p>";

?>

[PSR-2] You can also use <? = ...?> .

<?= "<p>Hola</p>" ?>

Comments

It is advised to use // in the comments of a single line.

The comments of several lines can be delimited with / * ... * / or with several // .

You should not use #.

To facilitate readability, it is advisable to place the comment closure of several lines (* /) at the beginning of the line (although it may be preceded by blank spaces).

```php
<?php
$nombre = "Fulano" // Nombre del individuo
?>
```

```php
<?php
/* Datos personales:
   Nombre, apellidos
*/
$nombre   = "Fulano"
$apellidos = "Mengánez Zutánez";
?>
```

```php
<?php
// Datos personales:
// Nombre, apellidos
$nombre   = "Fulano"
$apellidos = "Mengánez Zutánez";
?>
```

Initial comment blocks

[PEAR] Programs should include comment blocks (docblocks) at the beginning of the document.

```php
<?php
/**
* Descripción breve
*
* Descripción extensa (opcional)
*
* @author Fulanito de Tal <fulanito@example.com>
* @copyright 2007 Fulanito de Tal
* @license http://www.fsf.org/licensing/licenses/gpl.txt GPL 2 or later
* @version 2007-02-06
* @link http://www.example.org
*/
?>
```

To be completed: mention JavaDoc and phpDocumentor.

Line length

Do not exceed 85 characters per line.

When splitting a line, the second and subsequent lines must be bled 4 spaces. If possible, these lines should start with an operator.

```php
<?php

print "<p>Este texto es muy largo y no cabe en una sola línea, así que he "

    . "partido el texto en dos líneas escribiendo el operador de concatenación "

    . "(.) al principio de cada línea.</p>";

?>
```

Instructions by line

It is advisable not to include more than one instruction per line.

Blanks

[PEAR] After a comma, there must be a blank space.

```php
<? php
```

```
$ var = foo ( $ bar, $ cel, $ ona );

?>
```

[PEAR] Any binary operator (for example: + - * / =. == && ||?:) Must be surrounded by blanks.

```
<?php

$cmTotal = 100000 * $km + 100 * $m + $cm;

?>
```

[PEAR] Unary operators (for example:! ++ -) must join their argument without blanks

```
<?php

$correcto = !$error;

?>
```

Blank lines

It is advisable to separate the different parts of a program with blank lines (data collection, error messages, program response, etc.).

Double and simple quotes

It is advisable to delimit the strings with double quotes (") instead of single quotes ('). It is also advised that the HTML code generated by PHP include double quotes:

```php
<?php

print "<p style=\"text-align: center\">Hola</p>";

?>
```

Variable names

[PEAR] Variable names should be written with the camelCase style, that is, start in lowercase and, if the variable name consists of several words, the first letter of the words (except the first one) should be written in upper case

```php
$nombre        = "Fulano";

$nombreAlumno  = "Mengano";

$nombreProfesor = "Zutano";
```

Alignment of variable definitions

[PEAR] If several variables are defined, the equalities must be aligned with blank spaces to facilitate readability.

```php
$nombre        = "Fulano";

$nombreAlumno  = "Mengano";
```

```php
$nombreProfesor = "Zutano";
```

Note: This style is recommended in the PEAR style guide and discouraged in the Python style guide.

Constants

Constants should be written in uppercase and separating words with underscores (_).

The constants true, false, and null must be written in lowercase.

Bleeding

You must use a 4 space bleed and do not use tabs. In nested structures, the indentations will accumulate.

```php
<?php
if (condicion1) {
    accion1;
} else {
    accion2;
    if (condicion3) {
        accion3;
    } else {
```

```
    accion4;

  }

}

?>
```

Control structures

The control structures must have a space between the reserved word and the initial parenthesis, to distinguish them from the functions.

Keys should always be used in sentence blocks, even when they could be omitted (for example, when the block consists of a single statement). The opening key must be at the end of the line, and the closing key must be at the beginning of the line.

Examples of control structures:

```
<?php
if (condicion1 || condicion2) {

    accion1;

} elseif (condicion3 && condicion4) {

    accion2;
```

```php
} else {

  accionpredeterminada;

}

?>

for (expresión_inicial; expresión_final; expresión_paso) {

  bloque_de_sentencias

}

foreach ($matriz as $valor) {

  bloque_de_sentencias

}

while (expresión) {

  bloque_de_sentencias

}

do {

  bloque_de_sentencias

} while (expresión)

<?php

switch (condicion) {

case 1:
```

```
    accion1;

    break;


case 2:

    accion2;

    break;


default:

    accionpredeterminada;

    break;

}

?>
```

Logical expressions

It is not necessary to compare the Boolean variables with the values true or false; it is advisable to use the variable or its negation directly.

Instead of:

```
if ($correcto == true) {

    print "<p>Es correcto</p>";
```

```
}
if ($correcto == false) {

    print "<p>No es correcto</p>";

}
```

it is advisable to write:

```
if ($correcto) {

    print "<p>Es correcto</p>";

}
if (!$correcto) {

    print "<p>No es correcto</p>";

}
```

When concatenating simple logical expressions, it is not necessary to write each expression in parentheses.

```
if ($numero < 0 || $numero > 100) {

    print "<p>El número no está en el intervalo [0, 100]</p>";

}
```

Definition of functions

[PEAR] Functions must be declared according to the "BSD / Allman" style:

```php
<?php

function fooFuncion($arg1, $arg2 = "")

{

  if (condicion) {

    sentencia;

  }

  return $val;

}

?>
```

Arguments with default values must be placed at the end of the argument list.

The functions must return some value.

Calling functions

There should be no spaces between the name of the function, the initial parenthesis, and the first argument. There must be spaces after commas that separate arguments. There should be no spaces between the last argument, the final parenthesis, and the semicolon.

```php
<?php

$var = foo($bar, $cel, $ona);

?>
```

Libraries

[PEAR] To include libraries whose inclusion does not depend on any condition, use require_once and parentheses should not be used around the name of the library.

```php
require_once "biblioteca.php";

...
```

Recommendations not adopted

Included in this section are some recommendations from the PSR-2 and PEAR style guides not adopted in these notes.

File formats

[PEAR] Files should be saved in ASCII format and use ISO-8859-1 or UTF-8 encoding and Unix format (LF character as the end of the line and at the end of the last line of the file).

Error management

To complete.

Tools

PHP-Beautifier is a PEAR package that automatically formats PHP files.

PHP_CodeSniffer is a PEAR package that detects formatting errors in PHP files.

phpDocumentor is a PEAR package that detects formatting errors in PHP files.

CODING RULES AND PHP CODE GUIDELINES

Following the simple rules of this guide allows a better organization and productivity in the programming of projects in teams or alone. Many of these rules are based on the style guides of large free projects, such as phpBB.

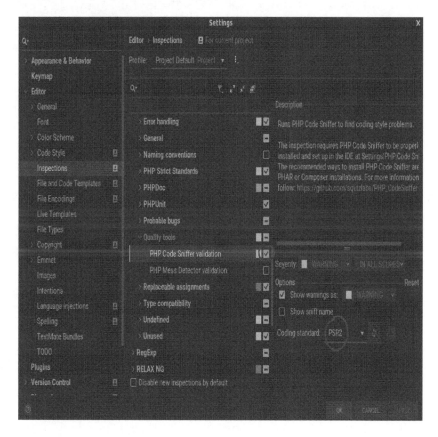

General standards

Tabs or Spaces.

In the content within brackets, this content will always be identified with tabs. Any decent editor can be configured to put tabs instead of spaces in the indentation (Dreamweaver, Aptana, Eclipse, etc.)

File header

It is always important that all .php files start with a specific header that indicates version information, author of the latest changes, etc. It is up to every team to decide whether or not to add more data

/ **

*

* @Control of presentation of the weblogs. "weblog.php"

* @ version: 5.4.2 @modified: September 1, 2006

* @autor: Freddie

*

* /

Comments on functions

All functions must have a comment, before their declaration, explaining what they do. No programmer should have to analyze the code of a function to know its usefulness. Both the name and the comment accompanying the function should suffice for this.

Lessons

Classes will be placed in a separate .php file, where only the class code will be placed. The name of the file will be the same as that of the class and will always start in upper case. If possible, ensure that class names have only one word.

The classes follow the same rules of the functions; therefore, a comment should be placed before the declaration of the class explaining its usefulness.

Hacks

The hacks that need to be placed in the code must, like the classes or functions, be commented on and, if possible, encourage other programmers to replace them or improve them for better solutions.

File location

In web projects or applications, the following folders will usually be available:

/ Root Folder: Here will go the .php files to which the user directly accesses, interface, etc.

classes: A folder containing exclusively the classes used in the project

includes: All files that are called by others .php in the form of modules or function libraries.

db: In case of having the possibility of using several databases, here we will place the .php that handle those multilayer characteristics for each supported data system.

templates: In case of using a template system (Like smarty or phpBB), here we will save all the .tpl files

PHP code style and rules

Variable names

As much as it seems the "coolest," it is recommended not to adopt the Hungarian notation in the code. This is the one where we put the data type before the variable name: strName for a string. As much as possible DO NOT use it, many large projects firmly believe that it is one of the most widely used code obfuscation techniques today.

The names must be descriptive and concise. Do not use big phrases or small abbreviations for the variables. It is always better to know what a variable does if you only know its name. This applies to the names of variables, functions, function arguments, and classes.

All the names must be in lowercase (Except with the classes, where the first letter must be uppercase). In case of using more than one word, it will be separated by an underscore sign " _."

In functions, it is important that the name denotes its function immediately. Things like print_data are fine, but it would be better to print_data_user. Similarly, in the arguments of the functions, we want to know immediately what we are using., It is better to create_user ($ nick, $ email) than create ($ n, $ e) .

The philosophy is simple. Do not damage the readability of the code due to laziness. Of course, apply common sense and do not create functions of more than 4 words.

Always include brackets

It's simple if you were going to do this:

if ($ thing) function ( ) ;

Better do this

if ($ thing)

{

　function ( ) ;

}

You do not spend much additional time, and you gain a lot in readability.

Brackets or keys Where to place them

Although this is a reason for constant fights in the work teams, it is best to follow the path that allows greater clarity in the development. To put it in a few words, all the brackets go in a proper line.

```
if ( something )

{

    for ( iteration )

    {

        // code

    }

}

while ( condition )

{

    function ( ) ;

}
```

Put spaces between signs

Another simple thing. If you have a binary sign, put spaces on both sides. You have a unary sign, put spaces on one side. Or in simpler terms, the program as if you wrote (well) in Spanish. It's something very simple that can help a lot in the reading of the code.

This is bad:

```php
$ a = 0 ;

for ( $ i = 5 ; $ i <= $ j ; $ i ++ )
```

This is good:

```php
$ a = 0 ;

for ( $ i = 5 ; $ i <= $ j ; $ i ++ )
```

Precedence of operators

You can be a hardcore programmer, but do you really know the precedence of operators in PHP? As we think not, it is best to always use parentheses to be sure. Basically, the idea is to not leave complex operations to mathematical freaks and be sure that our teammates with less "skill" understand everything without problems:

```php
// What the hell does this give as a result?
$ bool = ( $ i < 7 && $ j > 8 || $ k == 4 ) ;
```

```php
// On the other hand, if I put it that way, it is obvious and simple
$ bool = ( ( $ i < 7 ) && ( ( $ j < 8 ) || ( $ k == 4 ) ) ) ;
```

```php
// But this one is even better because it is more optimized and its
reading is higher
```

```
$ bool = ( $ i < 7 && ( $ j < 8 || $ k == 4 ) ) ;
```

Text strings in quotes

PHP has two ways to put strings or strings of text. With single quotes and double quotes. The difference is that if you use double quotes and insert a variable name into the text, the compiler will interpret it and replace it with its value. For this reason, you must always use single quotes unless you need to do the interpolation of variables that allow doubles. It's hard to get used to because it happens only in PHP (and some other more malignant ones, Perl4Life) but that's why it's PHP.

Of course, there are special cases where it is better to use double quotes (like when you use escape characters \ intensively) so feel free to break this rule when it is to improve the reading of the code.

Numbers within the code

Sometimes we put special numbers inside our code for special situations. DO NOT DO IT . If you need to put a special number, make it constant and then implement it. Example:

```
define ('ARTICLES_PORTED', 10);

for ( $ i = 0 ; $ i < ARTICULOS_PORTADA ; $ i ++ )

{
```

Unary operators of addition and subtraction.

It's simple, use them in a single line and on the right, example:

```
// This is BAD

$ thing = $ matrix [ $ i - ] ;

$ another = $ matrix [ ++ $ y ] ;


// This is OK

$ and ++;

$ thing = $ matrix [ $ i ] ;

$ another = $ matrix [ $ y ] ;

$ i -;
```

Conditional single-line

Use them only to do simple things. Whenever possible, always use if

```
// Only in these cases are

$ min = ( $ i < $ j ) valid ? $ i : $ j ;
```

Do not use variables without initializing

If you do not have control over the value of a variable, verify that it is initialized. This is allowed by PHP as follows:

```
// Bad fact:

if ( $ client == 5 ) ...
```

```
// Well done

if ( isset ( $ client ) && $ client == 5 ) ...
```

But only use this option when you do not have control or are not sure what value the variable can have (As in variables that arrive by parameter or by GET, etc.)

Instruction "switch."

This is one of the ugliest things in C style languages. When you should use it, try to follow the following style:

```
switch ( $ mode )

{

    case 'mode1' :

        // Success code

    break ;


    case 'modo2' :
```

```
    // Algorithm that will retire me at 25 years

break ;


default :

    // Code if everything fails

break ;

}
```

Not mandatory, but recommended.

The programming of PHP projects in a group is made much more effective by applying these rules. If you want to expand this information and know other guides such as rules to perform SQL queries, to create design templates or for other advanced cases, we invite you to read the Coding Guidelines of phpBB . In the same way, you can access our style guide in CSS for a similar document applied to the world of web design.

CODING STYLE GUIDE

This section extends the basic PSR-1 coding standard.

The objective of this section is to reduce the difficulty when reading code from different authors. It does this by enumerating a common set of rules and expressions on how to format PHP code.

The code MUST follow the PSR-1 standard.

The code MUST use 4 spaces as indentation, not tabs.

There MUST NOT be a strict limit on the length of the line; the limit MUST be in 120 characters; the lines SHOULD have 80 characters or less.

There MUST be a blank row after the statement namespace, and there MUST be a blank line after the declaration block use.

The opening keys for the classes MUST go on the next line, and the closing keys MUST go on the next line to the body of the class.

The opening keys of the methods MUST go on the next line, and the closing keys MUST go on the next line to the body of the method.

Visibility MUST be declared in all properties and methods; abstract and final must be declared before visibility; static must be declared after visibility.

The keywords of the control structures MUST have space after them, the calls to the methods and the functions MUST NOT have it.

The opening keys of the control structures MUST be on the same line, and the closing keys MUST go on the next line to the body.

The opening parentheses in the control structures MUST NOT have space after them, and the closing parentheses MUST NOT have space before them.

1.1. Example

This example includes some of the following rules as a quick overview:

```php
<?php

namespace Proveedor\Paquete;


use FooInterfaz;

use BarClase as Bar;

use OtroProveedor\OtroPaquete\BazClase;


class Foo extends Bar implements FooInterfaz
{
    public function funcionDeEjemplo($a, $b = null)
```

```
{

    if ($a === $b) {

        bar();

    } elseif ($a > $b) {

        $foo->bar($arg1);

    } else {

        BazClase::bar($arg2, $arg3);

    }

}


    final public static function bar()

    {

        // Cuerpo del método

    }

}
```

2. General

2.1 Basic standard coding

The code MUST follow the rules outlined in the PSR-1 standard.

2.2 Files

All PHP files Requirement use the Unix LF end of the line.

All PHP files MUST finish with a blank line.

The closing tag ?>MUST be omitted in files that only contain PHP code.

2.3. Lines

There MUST NOT be a strict limit on the length of the line.

The flexible limit of the line MUST be in 120 characters; Automatic style correctors MUST warn of this, but they MUST NOT produce errors.

The lines SHOULD NOT be greater than 80 characters; the longest lines of these 80 characters SHOULD be divided into multiple lines of no more than 80 characters each.

There should NOT be any blank spaces at the end of the lines that are not empty.

WHITE lines can be added to improve code reading and to indicate code blocks that are related.

There should not be more than one sentence per line.

2.4. Indentation

The code MUST use an indentation of 4 spaces, and MUST NOT use tabs for indentation.

Note: Using only the spaces, and not mixing spaces with tabs, helps to avoid problems with diffs, patches, histories, and annotations. The use of gaps also makes it easy to adjust the alignment between lines.

2.5. Keywords and true/ false/ null.

The Keywords of PHP must be lowercase.

PHP constants true, false, and nullMUST be in lowercase.

3. Namespace and declarations use

When present, there MUST be a blank line after declaring the namespace.

When present, all statements useMUST go after the declaration of the namespace.

There MUST be one use per statement.

There MUST be a blank line with the declaration block use.

For example:

```
<?php
```

namespace Proveedor\Paquete;

use FooClass;

use BarClase as Bar;

use OtroProveedor\OtroPaquete\BazClase;

// ... código PHP additional...

4. Classes, properties, and methods

The word "class" refers to all classes, interfaces, or traits.

4.1. Extensions and implementations

Keywords extend and should be reported in the same line as the name of the class.

The opening key of the class MUST go on the next line; the closing key MUST go on the next line to the body of the class.

<?php

namespace Proveedor\Paquete;

use FooClase;

use BarClase as Bar;

```php
use OtroProveedor\OtroPaquete\BazClase;


class NombreDeClase extends ClasePadre implements
\ArrayAccess, \Countable
{
    // constants, Propiedad, métodos
}
```

The list implements are divided into multiple lines, where the subsequent lines will be indented once. When executing so, the first item in the list MUST be on the next line, and there MUST be a single interface per line.

```php
<?php
namespace Proveedor\Paquete;


use FooClase;
use BarClase as Bar;
use OtroProveedor\OtroPaquete\BazClase;


class NombreDeClase extends ClasePadre implements
    \ArrayAccess,
```

\Countable,

\Serializable

{

// constantes, propiedades, métodos

}

4.2. Properties

Visibility MUST be declared on all properties.

The keyword varMUST NOT be used to declare a property.

DO NOT declare more than one property per sentence.

Property names should NOT use a hyphen as a prefix to indicate whether they are private or protected.

A property statement will look like this.

```php
<?php
namespace Proveedor\Paquete;

class NombreDeClase
{
    public $foo = null;
```

```
}
```

4.3. Methods

Visibility MUST be declared in all methods.

The names of the methods SHOULD NOT use a hyphen as a prefix to indicate whether they are private or protected.

Method names MUST NOT be declared with space after the method name. The opening key MUST be placed on its line, and the closing key MUST go on the next line to the body of the method. There MUST NOT be any space after the opening parenthesis, and there MUST NOT be any space before the closing parenthesis.

The declaration of a method will look like this. Notice the situation of parentheses, commas, spaces, and keys:

```php
<?php

namespace Proveedor\Paquete;


class NombreDeClase
{
    public function fooBarBaz($arg1, &$arg2, $arg3 = [])
```

```
    {

        // cuerpo del método

    }

}
```

4.4. Arguments of the methods

In the list of arguments, there MUST NOT be a space before each comma, and there MUST be a space after each comma.

The arguments with default values of the method MUST go to the end of the argument list.

```
<?php

namespace Proveedor\Paquete;


class NombreDeClase

{

    public function foo($arg1, &$arg2, $arg3 = [])

    {

        // cuerpo del método

    }
```

}

The list of arguments CAN be divided into multiple lines, where each line will be indented once. When divided in this way, the first argument MUST be on the next line, and there MUST be only one argument per line.

When the argument list is divided into several lines, the closing parenthesis and the opening key MUST be together on their line separated by a space.

```php
<?php

namespace Proveedor\Paquete;


class NombreDeClase
{
    public function metodoConNombreLargo(
        ClassTypeHint $arg1,
        &$arg2,
        array $arg3 = []
    ) {
        // cuerpo del método
    }
```

}

4.5. Abstract, final and static

When the statements are present abstract and final, MUST precede the visibility statement.

When the statement is present static, it MUST go after the visibility statement.

```php
<?php
namespace Proveedor\Paquete;

abstract class NombreDeClase
{
    protected static $foo;

    abstract protected function zim();

    final public static function bar()
    {
```

```
    // cuerpo del método

  }

}
```

4.6. Calls to methods and functions

When a call to a method or a function is made, there MUST NOT be a space between the name of the method or function and the opening parenthesis, there MUST NOT be a space behind the opening parenthesis, and there MUST NOT be a space before the opening. Closing parenthesis. In the discussion list, there MUST NOT be space before each comma, and there MUST be a space after each comma.

```
<?php

bar();

$foo->bar($arg1);

Foo::bar($arg2, $arg3);
```

The list of arguments CAN be divided into multiple lines, where each one is indented once. When this happens, the first argument MUST be on the next line, and there MUST be only one argument per line.

```
<?php

$foo->bar(
```

$argumentoLargo,

$argumentoMaslargo,

$argumentoTodaviaMasLargo

);

5. Control Structures

The style rules for the control structures are the following:

There MUST be a space after a control structure keyword.

There should NOT be spaces behind the opening parenthesis.

There MUST NOT be spaces before the closing parenthesis.

There MUST be a space between closing parentheses and the opening key.

The body of the control structure MUST be indented once.

The closing key MUST be on the next line at the end of the body.

The body of each construction MUST be enclosed in braces. This standardizes the appearance of structures and reduces the likelihood of adding errors as new lines are added to the body of the structure.

5.1. if, elseif,else

A structure will look like this. Look at the place of the parentheses, the spaces and the keys; and that else and else are in the same line as the closing keys of the previous body.

```php
<?php
if ($expr1) {
    // if cuerpo
} elseif ($expr2) {
    // elseif cuerpo
} else {
    // else cuerpo;
}
```

The keyword elseifSHOULD be used instead of else if so that all keywords in the structure are composed of single-term words.

5.2. Switch, case

A structure switch will look like this. Look at the place where the parentheses, spaces, and keys are. The keyword case must be indented once switch, and the keyword break or any other completion keyword MUST be indented to the same level as the body of the keyword case. There MUST be a comment like // no break when there is a case non-empty cascade.

```php
<?php
switch ($expr) {
    case 0:
        echo 'Primer case con break';
        break;
    case 1:
        echo 'Segundo case sin break en cascada';
        // no break
    case 2:
    case 3:
    case 4:
        echo 'Tercer case; con return en vez de break';
        return;
    default:
        echo 'Case por defecto';
        break;
}
```

5.3. While do while

An instruction while will look like this. Look at the place where the parentheses, spaces, and keys are.

```php
<?php

while ($expr) {

    // cuerpo de la estructura

}
```

Likewise, a sentence does while will look like this. Look at the place where the parentheses, spaces, and keys are.

```php
<?php

do {

    // cuerpo de la estructura;

} while ($expr);
```

5.4. for

A sentence will look like this. Look at the place where the parentheses, spaces, and keys appear.

```php
<?php
```

```php
for ($i = 0; $i < 10; $i++) {

    // cuerpo del for

}
```

5.5 For each

A sentence for each will look like this. Look at the place where the parentheses, spaces, and keys appear.

```php
<?php

foreach ($iterable as $key => $value) {

    // cuerpo foreach

}
```

5.6. Try, catch

A block tries catch will look like this. Look at the place where the parentheses, spaces, and keys appear.

```php
<?php

try {

    // cuerpo del try
```

```
} catch (PrimerTipoDeExcepcion $e) {

    // cuerpo catch

} catch (OtroTipoDeExcepcion $e) {

    // cuerpo catch

}
```

6. Closures

The closures MUST be declared with space after the keyword function and a space before and after the keyword use.

The opening key MUST go on the same line, and the closing key MUST go on the next line at the end of the body.

There MUST NOT be a space behind the opening parenthesis of the discussion list or variable list, and there MUST'NT be a space ere the closing parenthesis of the argument list or variable list.

In the list of arguments and the variable list, there MUST NOT be a space before each comma, and there MUST be a space after each comma.

The arguments of the closures with default values MUST go to the end of the list of arguments.

A statement of closure will look like this. Look at the place where the parentheses, commas, spaces, and keys appear.

```php
<?php

$closureConArgumentos = function ($arg1, $arg2) {

    // cuerpo

};
```

```php
$closureConArgumentosYVariables = function ($arg1, $arg2) use
($var1, $var2) {

    // cuerpo

};
```

The list of arguments and the list of variables CAN be divided into multiple lines, where each new line will be indented once. When this happens, the first item in the list MUST go on a new line, and there MUST be only one case or variable per line.

When the list of arguments or variables is divided into several lines, the closing parenthesis and the opening key MUST be together on their line separated by a space.

Below are examples of closures with and without a list of arguments and variables, as well as with lists of arguments and variables in multiple lines.

```php
<?php

$listaLargaDeArgumentos_sinVariables = function (
```

```php
    $argumentoLargo,

    $argumentoMasLargo,

    $argumentoMuchoMasLargo

) {

    // cuerpo

};


$sinArgumentos_listaLargaDeVariables = function () use (

    $variableLarga1,

    $variableMasLarga2,

    $variableMuchoMasLarga3

) {

    // cuerpo

};


$listaLargaDeArgumentos_listaLargaDeVariables = function (

    $argumentoLargo,

    $argumentoMasLargo,

    $argumentoMuchoMasLargo
```

```php
) use (
    $variableLarga1,
    $variableMasLarga2,
    $variableMuchoMasLarga3
) {
    // cuerpo
};


$listaLargaDeArgumentos_listaDeVars = function (
    $argumentoLargo,
    $argumentoMasLargo,
    $argumentoMuchoMasLargo
) use ($var1) {
    // cuerpo
};
$listaDeArgumentos_listaLargaDeVariables = function ($arg) use (
    $variableLarga1,
    $variableMasLarga2,
    $variableMuchoMasLarga3
```

```
) {

    // cuerpo

};
```

Note that the formatting rules are also applied when a closure is used directly in a function or when the method is called as an argument.

```
<?php

$foo->bar(

    $arg1,

    function ($arg2) use ($var1) {

        // cuerpo

    },

    $arg3

);
```

7. Conclusion

There are many style elements, and practices intentionally omitted from this guide. These include but are not limited to:

Declarations of variables and global constants.

Declaration of functions.

Operators and assignments.

Alignment between lines.

Comments and documentation blocks.

Prefixes and suffixes in class names.

Good practices.

Future recommendations CAN review and extend this guide to address these or other elements of style and practice.

DATA CODING: A UTF-8 GUIDE FOR PHP AND MYSQL

If you are a PHP or MySQL developer, once you pass beyond the confines of comfortable English-only character sets, you find yourself quickly enmeshed in the wonderfully strange world of UTF-8.

A Quick Look UTF-8 Primer

Unicode is a widely used computer industry standard, which defines a complete mapping of unique values of numeric codes to the characters of most character sets written today, to help with systems interoperability and interchange of data.

UTF-8 is variable amplitude encoding (variable-width encoding) that can represent all the characters in the Unicode character set. It was designed to maintain backward compatibility with ASCII and to avoid complications with Endianness and byte position marks in UTF-16 and UTF-32. UTF-8 has enhanced the dominant character encoding for the World Wide Web, representing higher than half of all Web pages.

UTF-8 encodes every character using one to four bytes. The first 128 Unicode characters correspond one to one with ASCII, making the ASCII text valid, as well as the UTF-8, encoded text. It is for this purpose that systems that are limited to the use of the English character set are isolated from the complexities that may otherwise arise with UTF-8.

For example, the Unicode hexadecimal code for the letter A is U + 0041, which in UTF -8 is simply encoded with the single byte 41. In comparison, the Unicode hexadecimal code for the character 丕 is U + 233B4, which in UTF-8 it is coded with the four bytes F0, A3, B4, 8E.

HP and the UTF-8 Coding - Modifications in the php.ini File:

The primary thing you should do is change your 'php.ini' file to use UTF-8 as the default character set:

default_charset = "utf-8";

(Note: You can later use phpinfo () to verify that it has been set correctly).

Well, now PHP and UTF-8 should work well together. True?

Well, not exactly. They are not close to doing it.

While this change will ensure that PHP will always output to UTF-8 as the character encoding (in browser-type content-response headers), you still have to make several modifications to your PHP code, to make sure that processes and generates UTF-8 characters correctly.

CONCLUSION

PHP is an open-source programming language on the server side that is used primarily to create dynamic web pages. The abbreviation was originally from "Personal Home Page Tools," although nowadays it has become the recursive acronym for " PHP: Hypertext Preprocessor."

While the client-side languages such as HTML, CSS, or JavaScript are interpreted first by the web browser at the time of opening a page, the PHP code runs on the web server. There, the PHP scripts generate the HTML code that is then sent to the browser. This does not receive the real code (the PHP script), but the result of the execution of it.

The main application scope of PHP is server-side programming, especially of dynamic pages and applications. Other areas of implementation are the creation of desktop applications or the programming of command lines. Despite having a simple syntax for beginners, PHP offers a remarkable number of functions. Its extensive support distinguishes this programming language to databases, it can be used in all types of platforms and is covered by a special PHP license that allows its free use and modification of the source code, a combination that is more than convincing.

It should be noted that four of the most popular content management systems, namely WordPress, TYPO3, Joomla, and Drupal, are based on PHP. A market analysis of W3Techs states that this scripting language is used in 82.4 percent of all World Wide Web pages (data as of February 1, 2017), which indicates that PHP is, by far, the common popular server-side programming language in the framework of web development. This becomes enough reason for more and more users to become familiar with the possibilities of PHP: Hypertext Preprocessor.

PHP tutorial is aimed at beginners and can be considered as an initiation into the world of server-side programming. However, many examples presuppose certain knowledge of the fundamentals of web development. It is also expedient to familiarize yourself with the HTML markup language first.

The fastest way to learn PHP is by understanding the examples and adapting them to the needs of each web project. All that is needed for programming with PHP is a web server with a PHP interpreter, a text editor (for instance, Notepad ++ or Vim) and a web browser. As a server for a first inclusion, it is recommended to use the XAMPP local test environment, made available by Apache Friends for Windows, Linux, and macOS operating systems free of charge.

PHP